Between high and low water

Also by Jan Sutch Pickard and published by Wild Goose:

Dandelions and Thistles
Out of Iona
Advent Readings from Iona (with Brian Woodcock)

Between h low wai

Sojourner sor

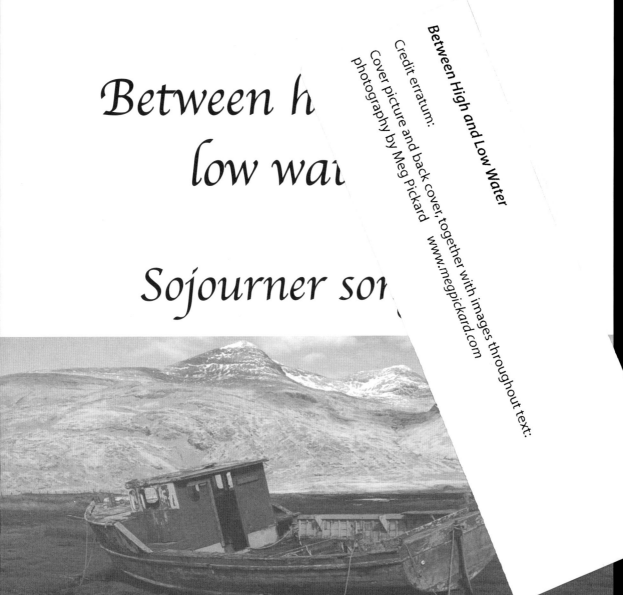

Jan Sutch Pickard

WILD GOOSE PUBLICATIONS

Between High and Low Water

Credit erratum:
Cover picture and back cover, together with images throughout text:
photography by Meg Pickard   www.megpickard.com

Copyright © 2008, Jan Sutch Pickard

First published by Wild Goose Publications, 2008
4th Floor, Savoy House, 140 Sauchiehall St, Glasgow G2 3DH, UK.
Wild Goose Publications is the publishing division of the Iona Community.
Scottish Charity No. SCO03794. Limited Company Reg. No. SCO96243.
www.ionabooks.com

ISBN 978 1 905010 45 5

**The publishers gratefully acknowledge the support of the Drummond Trust,
3 Pitt Terrace, Stirling FK8 2EY in producing this book.**

Overseas distribution:
Australia: Willow Connection Pty Ltd, Unit 4A, 3–9 Kenneth Road, Manly Vale, NSW 2093
New Zealand: Pleroma, Higginson Street, Otane 4170, Central Hawkes Bay
Canada: Novalis/Bayard, 10 Lower Spadina Ave., Suite 400, Toronto, Ontario M5V 2Z

A catalogue record for this book is available from the British Library.

Printed by Thomson Litho, East Kilbride, UK

Contents

Letting go ... and holding on

Figures in a landscape

Conversations with Attie

In this very place

Odd shoes

Another landscape

Not cursing the darkness

Appendices

Introduction

I am a sojourner – that's a beautiful and ancient word, but what does it mean today? I live on the island of Mull, in a community where many of my neighbours have deep roots, whereas I grew up in a family constantly on the move. Here, I'll always be an incomer. Folk are accepting; I hope to become a contributing member of the community; at the same time I know I belong to a wider world. Travelling away, from time to time, I come back with stories of other landscapes, communities and cultures, to set alongside those that belong on the Ross of Mull. Outsiders are expected to ask awkward questions, so I do, sometimes. In return, my neighbours, while making me welcome, ask, 'Will you stay? Can you ever settle down, or are you just passing through?' In the church as much as in the village street, I know I'm an incomer, a bird of passage, a resident alien, one who makes a temporary stay among others: a sojourner.

In common with many folk at the beginning of the twenty-first century, I'm living across cultures, and sometimes, as a Christian, counter-culturally. We find ourselves in a time of transition, between the tides of history. So the expanse of the foreshore – where I walk most days – is a powerful symbol for me: it is open to constant change, the stones and wrack swept in and out, sandbanks reconfigured, moving waters, restless flights of birds.

Moreover, I've learned from my mentors in Mull, particularly Attie MacKechnie and Bill Pollock, that between high and low water was one of the few places – out of the jurisdiction of the established Church and the power of the landlords – where dissident preachers could gather their congregations. In their time they were 'voices in the wilderness', speaking out for justice. They walked with the many people of faith through the centuries who (in the words of the Letter to the Hebrews) 'acknowledged themselves to be strangers and aliens without fixed abode on earth'. Inspiring, but maybe not easy folk to be with!

I'm also a Member of the Iona Community, a dispersed community, a radical movement among the churches of people who try to live the Gospel while finding it profoundly unsettling. We believe

> *'that the Gospel commands us to seek peace founded on justice,*
> *that costly reconciliation is at the heart of the Gospel;*

and that work for justice, peace and an equitable society
is a matter of extreme urgency.'
(from the Iona Community Justice and Peace Commitment)

Five years ago, Wild Goose published *Out of Iona*, which drew on experiences
of living in community and working in the Abbey and MacLeod Centre,
together with ways that the Community's Justice and Peace Commitment
compelled me to engage with the wider world.

Since leaving Iona, I have had a chance to live in very different communities,
from a university campus in London, to the West Bank and back to a small
village in the West of Scotland. When I went to the West Bank Palestinian
Territories as a volunteer with the Ecumenical Accompaniment Programme in
Palestine and Israel, the task included monitoring and advocacy: writing reports
and articles; but sometimes only poetry could express the experience. Here in
Mull, as a storyteller and lay preacher, I speak aloud as often as I write things
down. Sometimes I walk the shore, struggling for the right words – and find
them playing in the air around me.

Scribe on the shore

The waves roll
toward the shore –
line by line.

A flock of small birds
wheels dark above,

                    changes direction
        with a shimmer of white
        and lands

in a different
pattern
        on each page.

I want to celebrate the swing of the tides and the circle of the seasons, to enjoy and explore the uniqueness of places. My sojourner songs are written to honour folk who know these places as home; for those with whom I've shared meals and vigils, conversations and laughter; and to honour those others, moved by the urgency of justice and peace, whom I meet on the margins, in the windswept spaces 'between high and low water'.

Many of these poems have already appeared in print, in a series of small pamphlets called **Gatherings** *(the name is explained on p. 24)*, produced with the idea that people find poetry in small quantities less intimidating! There was a reason for producing each pamphlet: a sabbatical spent visiting libraries and looking at mediaeval manuscripts; the experience of leaving Iona (which some of you reading this will have shared); a brief but very focused visit to the Holy Land, then a longer period living and working there as an Ecumenical Accompanier. Some were written as messages of encouragement to friends and companions, others are a way of reflecting on questions from complex experience. Sometimes I was singing to myself; sometimes, in the face of injustice, wanting to make a public statement – to be performed, or posted on walls to catch the eye of passers-by.

The first sequence was written after taking part in an all-night vigil in the heart of London. It's a call to action – so why not begin with 'Waking up Whitehall'?

Jan Sutch Pickard

Waking up Whitehall

Why we're here

To sit on the chill stone floor
in an ancient church
and listen to voices from the two-thirds world;
to listen to questions
to share anger
to express hope –
that's why we're here.
It makes up for all those righteous pews,
comfy chairs
and politeness.
It's why we're who we are,
in all our cheerful diversity.

To stand shoulder to shoulder,
moved, moving,
on the edge of dancing
to African drumming
which echoes from the vaulted roof
and rocks the walls of the Abbey –
that makes sense
of churchgoing.
It reminds us
of who we are:
the people of God on the move.

To be encouraged, excited,
incited to take to the streets;
to go out of that grand doorway,
like royalty, the common people,
together and one by one;
to leave in a great wave
like the start of a marathon –
with a message
for the people in power –
this makes sense;
it's why we're here,
doing our best to be
the human race.

Vigil – images

Having carried their little lights
from all corners of the kingdom –
lanterns and torches and church candles
and household candles in jars from under the stairs –
they share matches to light them,
awkwardly.
The last time they did this was a power cut:
but this is more of a power surge.

***

Where, on most days,
passers-by are asked for change,
tonight all who pass by
are offered a candle
to light
to hold
to make a difference,
to bring about change.

***

As though crocuses
had burst through the concrete
and into bloom, all down Whitehall
the candles are lit.

***

Your hands cradle a flame
in a homely jam jar:
the night wind cannot shake it.
Although you tremble
with the strangeness
of being here,
your eyes are steady.

***

A great crowd keeping silence.
Actions speak louder than words.
This is deafening.

Were you there?

(At 11.45pm, there was one minute's silence)

Were you there for the silence?
Some of us were streets away
but the silence rolled towards us,
with its own power, and impelled
by the outcry and cheering that followed.

The sound, human; the silence, God-with-us.
Can silence be measured? It goes on.
Listen, it is still there, around, within,
wherever we are: whether or not
we are there for the silence –
the silence is there for us.

Stars, angels

In St Margaret's Church
look up – there are angels
from one end to the other.
But only those towards the east
are gilded.

Over our heads
there are stars, too, moulded into the plaster
where roof beams intersect, setting worship
among the singing spheres.
But only those over the chancel
are gilded.

You stand up at the east end,
in the big spaces of this building,
facing a great field of folk
shepherded into pews –
a small shy angel – and you get us
all singing.

How can we be sheepish
when you shine with encouragement?
'You can do it … Cool!' – so we all shine,
and the sound we make is heaven-sent,
unites the church,
tickles the angels,
shakes the stars.

We're transcending, with God's grace,
the hierarchy that fallen human beings
keep putting into place.
You remind us how amazing we are –
that when we sing we're all pure gold:
we're all angels,
we're all stars.

Embankment

It was a long night; the vigil kept on going;
the crowds ebbed and flowed, tired now,
lugging their big banners, cherishing little lights.

When it became too painful to stand still
I walked the wakeful streets: partygoers,
police, rough sleepers, newspaper vans,
lorries with milk and bread, life going on,
but disconnected. I came to the river

and near the sleeping cyclops of the Eye
I stood, watching the tidal Thames
unfurling itself like a dark silken banner,
stitched with symbols and manifestos –
unreadable in the dark hours. Stubbornly
went on with this night-watch, intimidated
by the traffic's random roar; went on waiting,
wondering why I was there, while sane folk slept.

Then heard a tentative voice over my head
in the dark branches, another answering,
and more and more, declaring to the city
a different way of being: call it hope,
community, connectedness? No, I wept
because, right then, I couldn't find the words
for the first inklings of dawn in the sky
and all the trees of London full of birds.

Wake-up call

So you all gathered
in one place
at the heart of the city –
the cold heart –
in the place where power is located,
at 4am,
the time when the world is most awake.
So you all gathered.
And then?
Then you made a big noise –
what was it like?
Uninhibited?
Threatening?
Hilarious?
Heartening?
What noise did you make?
What difference will it make?

Now I'm listening, to find out.

Go on, I want to hear
a noise that would wake politicians
from their complacency
and our nation out of its apathy
and shake the institutions.
Make that noise!

Only if you join in.

Bananas

At 5am the stewards brought out bananas –
big boxes
of organic fairtrade fruit –
offered freely
handed out,
handed round
tossed to the hands of the hungry crowd.

Surprised
and sharing
we found they were just what we needed:
cold and sweet:
as cold as the streets
as sweet as justice.

A gathering

Introduction

A gathering is a piece of parchment, folded and cut to make sixteen pages or eight spreads – the basic unit of a mediaeval manuscript. This is a nugget of information which might not seem very applicable to daily life in the twenty-first century, even in Iona, almost certainly the birthplace of the Book of Kells.

When I was Warden of Iona Abbey, I was given a sabbatical, six weeks at the end of the 2002 season. I decided to learn more about the kind of manuscripts that had been copied with such loving care, treasured and used for worship by generations of monks on Iona: first Columba and his followers, 1500 years ago, and then their Benedictine successors, from 1200 until the Reformation. Since the Abbey in Iona lay in ruins for several centuries after that, I'd have to visit other libraries, like the one in St Gallen, in Switzerland, which have been centres of learning for hundreds of years. The manuscripts in St Gallen include the handiwork of wandering Irish monks who lived on the island of Reichenau, on a lake in the heart of Europe, at the same time as their brothers in faraway Iona. And of course the journey took me to Trinity College Dublin, drawn by the jewel-bright colours and intricate designs of the Book of Kells.

But what is the relevance of this to living and working in Iona today, welcoming wanderers from all over the world, and relating to the issues of that world? I left Iona as the library there was being packed up, because the buildings were being rewired. In the time of the Viking raids, a whole library was lost in Iona. As I was writing, a national library went up in flames in Baghdad. What would it mean to live in a world where learning is under attack; a world without books, even?

As I looked at these ancient artefacts in glass cases, deciphering the Latin words, or called them up on computer screens, or even (in Chetham's Library, Manchester) turned the pages of a fourteenth-century missal, I felt the presence of the fellow Christians who made them, the craft skills, creativity and stubborn faith these books represented. I was reminded of the power of words and imagination, even in our chaotic world, and of my own faith in a God who is the living and life-giving Word.

Abbey library
(October 2002)

The shelves are eating the books –
said the librarian,
who is trained in these things.

Static shelving, grained and gracious oak
seeming set for all time,
is in fact in flux:
dead vegetable matter, breaking down,
releasing gases, to make the old books
more brittle still, till they crumble
like leaves on the forest floor.

They would be far safer –
she said –
in steel stacks.

Meanwhile, I stand
as though in an enchanted wood,
breathing the books' autumnal fragrance:
having proof now
that, through all its perils,
this library is alive.

Packing up the library

To lose one library
is a misfortune; to lose two
looks like carelessness.
So, before the Abbey is rewired,
the books are on the move –
going into the ark two by two:
into the archive boxes.
Lying down meekly –
the lion with the lamb,
polemic with peace studies,
poetry with politics,
Celtic studies with eschatology;
gathered in from the open shelves
where saint and sinner
were free to browse.

Now safe and unread under hatches
while the rain falls on a wordless world
till the dove sounds the all-clear.

Silence

Just as the snowdrop needs frost
to rest and to germinate,
so libraries need silence:

stacks of silent tomes
hushed scholars
whispered instructions
slippered feet, gloved hands,
muted computers.

Sometimes libraries surprise
with unlikely acquisitions:
a snoozing tramp amid newspapers;
eloquent love letters, penned
by hands long since crumbled into dust;
a harp not played in living hearing;
mummy cases opened like Russian dolls,
disclosing the child of an Egyptian priest
clenched in an aching silence.

What have these to do with books,
and the lively faith of their makers
whose daily work was sowing
symbols across the page?

What have these relics to do
with meaning coming through
like a green shoot –
entering our minds like a flight of birds?

Taciturn and tired folk, things worn out,
exhale the dead air of a treasure house;
meanwhile the held breath of a library
is not the silence of death
but of expectation.

The books are waiting for what will come next:
the books are waiting for the word to become flesh.

Appointment with a missal

The train was late,
but you had been waiting
for more than six hundred years.

It was a strangely formal meeting:
I brought my references,
you came with a full CV.

On the polished table
lay white gloves;
you seemed larger than life.

A wary encounter, because hands-on:
before now your beauty
has been crudely put-upon –

first respected, then raped:
your finest jewels coveted
by ignorant folk, your story confused;

your soft skin bruised,
bearing the scars
of unkind cuts, uncouth greed, disbelief.

Yet in spite of all you have been through
and my impertinent questions,
our disparities of language and age,

you courteously gave me your full attention
for the space of two hours –
touching me with the turning of each page.

Meeting your dogged faithfulness face-to-face,
I learned with the gloves off
about tough love – and grace.

November

The story of the year,
the lore of growing trees –
recorded in brown and golden leaves –
is falling all around us now:
falling on a tired world, on far green islands
and in grey traffic-bound cities,
on grimy streets, on parked cars,
in London squares, in courtyards of libraries,
falling outside the windows of long rooms:
where the books
which have fallen out of the remote past
have come to rest.

Abbot Heito

'Wise in counsel, devout of spirit, cheerful in speech,
possessing a believing heart,
and as full of wisdom as a chest full of books.'

Abbot Heito, on the island of Reichenau,
in the so-called Dark Ages,
possessed a believing heart (how could he survive otherwise?)
and expressed his hands-on faith
by building a basilica over the bones of a gospel writer;
built a community of scholars like himself
on the green island (were they cheerful too?)
gathered skilled scribes and gathered the written word –
revered relics and working documents –
in Greek and Latin, Arabic and Gaelic,
gathered up books by the chest-full.

But now, in our enlightened age,
the books are bound for no other destination:
they are all dressed up with nowhere to go:
in tooled and gilded bindings, all the hues of autumn leaves,
artefacts hoarded, in cases locked against thieves.
There is even a labyrinth on the library floor
which we must trace to find the treasure.

Abbot Heito, in his different world,
was as full of wisdom as a chest full of books.
But where a chest contains, stores and keeps safe,
his story (as far as we can tell at this distance)
is about a way of being that embodied God's love,
and broke to share it, becoming a resource:
for the known world:
the chest open
        the book open
                the word living.

Ultramarine

(When the Book of Kells was written, there was only one known source of the lapis lazuli that was used in its decoration: a mine in the mountains of north-west Afghanistan.)

Ultramarine:
blue from beyond the sea –
rich blue, of Hebridean seas
which range from indigo to jade,
inlaid with rock and kelp, reflecting summer skies;
here the sea colours play upon a page
as white as sand,
where even waves fall on a distant strand
beyond the sea.

Ultramarine
was never meant to be a colour scheme.
The sea meant all that severs *us* from *them*,
and sometimes us from God:
remoteness, mountains, deep mines, desert plains,
warfare and trade, babel and otherness;
conjuring up camel trains and chartered ships
to carry, over land and over sea,
mineral wealth bought at a human price:
the ore of distant mines, a fist
clenching what was most rare – lapis lazuli –
blue from beyond the sea.

Ultramarine, lapis lazuli –
colours playing upon the page –
flickering blue like driftwood's salty flames,
in borders interlaced like fronds of kelp,
singling out angels, saints, fantastic birds,
and here the cloak of an evangelist.
The makers of this book
took blue from far beyond the world they knew
to hint at heaven.

Computer calligraphy

Call me insular
but I think one typeface will do me –

probably Arial,
sans serif, no frills,
pulled out of the air, and off the menu,
selected to communicate clearly
without giving the different messages
of *Edwardian*
or **Rockwell Extra Bold**
or MATISSE
or COPPERPLATE GOTHIC BOLD
or Σψμβολ (which is Greek to me)
and certainly without playing about with Curlz.

Oddly enough, this state-of-the-art computer
doesn't have Uncial –
that overused script
appearing now on a gift shop near you,
hinting at things ancient, crafty, collectable,
and lettered Celtic through and through
(it's on our letterhead too).

So here I am, on a dark December day,
on a remote island, at my desk,
playing with words and with letterforms,
as I try to imagine the size of the task, think
of the patience needed to write out the Gospel:
of lives as disciplined as lines ruled,

on the prepared parchment; of the armoury
of sharpened quills and the chemistry of ink …
by skill of pen-stroke, willing books into being:
forming them, letter by letter, word by word
in the hand we call insular majuscule.

Cheap grace, to conjure up, at the touch of a key,
the cramped handiwork of centuries gone,
creation that lasted days and months and years,
mindset of craftsmen giving to God
the stubborn slog, the costly task of lost community.

Yet even today, with all this technology
at my fingertips, it is not too late:
what still makes sense is finding the words that sing,
being hands-on in getting them down:
the scribe and I both, driven like the beat of birds' wings
by the need to communicate.

Chester Beatty MS

Like an urgent message
on the back of an envelope
this papyrus fragment
records Jesus' words from the cross:
'Woman, behold your son.'
It was written only 50 years
after the death of John,
that beloved friend, adopted son, solitary scribe
who gives his name to the gospel –
from which this handful of words
has come crumpled
out of the back pocket of time.

Easter hymn

God-given glory – resurrection dawn –
Tell the world the story, hope has been reborn.
Evermore God-with-us, as the light of day
Breaks into the tomb, the stone is rolled away:
> Yours is the glory! Glory, risen Lord!
> Out of death's dark silence comes the living Word.

Greet him, our Saviour, call him Jesus, Friend,
Teacher, Guide and Healer: doubt is at an end.
Celebrate his presence, people of one God,
And with ceaseless joy share good news with the world:
> Yours is the glory! Glory, risen Lord!
> Out of death's dark silence comes the living Word.

No more despair: we meet on common ground
Jesus, Prince of Peace, whose love is all around.
In the waves of conflict, courage – he is near;
Living in his presence, we're set free from fear:
> Yours is the glory! Glory, risen Lord!
> Out of death's dark silence comes the living Word.

(After the French of E. Bury, 1854–1932; as sung in Iona at Easter, 2003)

Holy places

Introduction

De Locis Sanctis (On the Holy Places) was the title of a book written by Adomnán, ninth Abbot of Iona and best known as Columba's biographer. About 100 years after the death of Columba, Adomnán and his community welcomed a pilgrim, Arculf. Iona was not his intended destination. He had been to the Holy Land, and on his way home to mainland Europe was blown a long way off course, arriving in Iona. In return for food and shelter, he told the Celtic monks the story of his journey, and about the places he had seen. Although Adomnán had never been there, he wanted to communicate this eyewitness account. So he wrote down in Latin all he had heard. He commented that there were many demands in his daily life as Abbot (life in community hasn't changed!) but this was just as important. He added other fragments of information and scholarship, and carried the book with him when he went to visit other communities.

In 2004 it was 1,300 years since the death of Adomnán, most of whose ministry was on the island of Iona, in his time already seen as a 'holy place' where pilgrims also came. But the encounter with Arculf, the account of a pilgrimage to the Holy Land, stimulated his imagination and challenged him to share his faith in a different way. In 2004 another encounter took place. A small group of people, Members and Youth Associates of the Iona Community (including myself as Warden of Iona Abbey), travelled to Jerusalem and the West Bank. We were pilgrims – that was what it said on our documents – going to visit the holy sites. But we were going at the invitation of Palestinian young people, to meet them, learn about their situation, pray with them.

It was a pilgrimage with a difference, for while the ancient streets and churches – the stones – could speak to us of faith in one way, we were able to meet local Christians – the 'living stones' of that land. We also met devout Muslim students, and radical Israelis who described themselves as atheists, alienated by all that was being done in the name of religion in that land. We were challenged by meeting people who did not want to take sides against each other, but against injustice, in a land being savagely divided by fences, by a huge wall, by prejudice and fear.

We saw sapling olive trees being planted close to the electrified fence, as a way of keeping hope alive. It is suffering and hope that makes this land holy. God is found in the courage and caring of ordinary people. Their hearts are the true Holy Places.

A world away

(for Adomnán)

Stones you never trod
cried out to you
as you paced these cobbles.

The winter gales brought a new order to the shore –
the pebbles sang together,
clattering like prayer beads.

As you chanted psalms on the sea's edge
your mind was turning over
names of far cities like incantations.

An unexpected guest, driven off course
and storm-stayed on Iona,
Arculf brought this gift from the sea:

the story of his quest, his pilgrimage,
and of the Holy Places: his words
rare and precious as ultramarine.

And though the busyness of the day
came at you from all quarters,
you had no choice but to set this down:

at second hand, your language intricate –
common words would not do –
imagined shrines glittered like mica.

So, a whole world away,
compelled by faith, you shared
the urgent message that the stones cried out.

Via Dolorosa

In the Old City
we read the inscriptions,
pause where a plaque on the wall
reminds us that Jesus falls
under the weight of the cross
over and over again.

In the refugee camp
we read the writing on the wall:
the stencilled images of martyrs,
graffiti, dusty posters,
calls to action, cries of pain
over and over again.

Women at the wall

At the Wailing Wall, women
hidden behind a wattle fence
reach across to touch
the scroll of the Law.

On the West Bank
there is another fence
topped with razor wire –

but there is no reaching over this barrier,
no appeal to the law that put it there.

Church of the Holy Sepulchre

All under one roof
like a religious shopping mall –
and as oppressive –
Calvary
and the Tomb
and the baffled common people
struggling up steps,
ducking through doorways,
lit by flickering lamps
each of which belongs
to a separate denomination.

A structure oppressive with power,
marked out into territories,
guarded by monks:
gloomy acres of space
patrolled by clergy in robes
and tour guides with worried flocks.

But what is at its heart?
Where would the people of God gather
who stray through the gloom
longing for meaning?

Such a pompous place,
such a weight of sadness,
so much history,
such disconnection
from what is happening in the streets –
such terrifying emptiness.

Why do we search for the living among the dead?

Church of the Nativity

There, shut away from the light of day,
men guard the empty tomb against rivals.

Here, through a low door,
becoming like children,
we enter a warm place.
Sunlight slants through high windows
and dust-motes dance,
light as the human spirit.
A woman, sweeping the patterned floor
with simple grace,
looks up, smiles, welcoming us
into a silent and expectant space.

St Peter Gallicantu

A church built on rock
at the sign of the crowing cock:
beside a worn flight of steps,
a place to stop and take stock.

Here, in the sanctuary,
rock juts out – powerful,
an undeniable statement of faith,
rugged, reliable –
but underneath, deep as doubt,
hollow dungeons and pits.

Close to the steps that Jesus trod
this hollow place is a hallowed place:
and still a hard place
to face yourself
            or to meet God.

Bells over Jerusalem

Sound, bell
Sound, bell
Clangour from one campanile among minarets
Sound, bell
Sound, bell
Resonance rolls round domes and out over the city
Sound, bell
Sound, bell
Swifts swoop and scream over dusty rooftops
Sound, bell
Sound, bell
Barbaric improvisation breaching an uneasy peace
Sound, bell
Sound, bell
Ponderous dance of giants in a city of myth
Sound, bell
Sound, bell
Like sounding brass or a clanging cymbal
Sound, bell
Sound, bell
Full of sound and fury, signifying nothing
Sound, bell
Sound, bell
Heartbeat of faith and arrhythmia of our times
Sound, bell
Sound, bell
A white dove circles, circles, but will not land
Sound   Bell
                    Sound   Bell
                                  Sound

The wall of separation

(Two haiku)

Behind it
real lives are invisible:
the blank face of denial.

***

Geology of oppression:
a scar
would take an earthquake to shift.

Hitting the wall

There are so many good reasons
to keep on going:
life is not a race, but I was into my stride,
had found a pace that would carry me for miles –
the adrenaline kept flowing –
and then I came to the wall.

It was huge, heart-stopping.
It shut out the sky.
And it said No.
No way.
No hope:
you can't pretend I'm not here –
here to stay –
and I came to a full stop.

There are so many reasons
to keep on going
and becoming fully alive:
up to now, wholeheartedly,
I lived them all –
until I hit the wall.

You need to be a bit crazy

(For Victoria, Israeli human rights activist, whose words below are in italics)

You don't need hope
to try to do the right thing.

You need to be a bit crazy
and angry with the men in power –
angry almost beyond words –
but it helps to hurl words at them,
to write your passionate NO on the dividing wall.

And despairing – does it help
to be despairing? as you see
the gradual grinding down to dust
of an occupied people,
and the complacency, the self-deception,
of their oppressors:

as you sit at the roadblock
watching a joyful wedding party
brought to a full-stop and, one by one,
put through the humiliating ceremony
of checking their IDs: It's a great way
to turn a decent person into a terrorist.

Pitying, too, *the poor teenage conscript*
who thinks he's preventing terrorism:
human beings not knowing which way to turn
from the roar and surge of the sea –
drowning in politics, dragging each other down.

It's not good for your peace of mind
to open your eyes, to keep watch.
It's not easy to be open-minded.
It's not sensible to open your mouth, to witness.
But it is necessary.

You call yourself *crazy*, and say
that long ago you *lost faith in religion*.
Yet though you cannot believe in God,
these are God-fearing acts.

You don't need hope
to try to do the right thing.

The flowers of the field

The poppy, the anemone –
blooming now after the spring rains –
they are different,
but both are as red as blood:

scattered across hillsides
where settlers' children play,
cared for by teachers carrying guns;

fragile among the rubble
where bulldozers groan
and fatherless children throw stones;

and when the wall is built,
they will still be flowering on both sides,
fragile as human lives –
different, but both red as blood.

Letting go ... and holding on

Introduction

Times of transition: one was leaving Iona where I lived, worshipped and worked in community for five and a half years. The rich experience and daily demands of that time were the ingredients for 'The heat of the kitchen', written for the then Abbey cook. Those who've stayed there for a week, or volunteered for a summer season, will recognise the finality of the ferry ramp going up ('Jetty waking').

These islands where I am writing can seem remote, but in surprising and subversive ways they are part of a wider world. Imagine George Orwell in a remote farmhouse on Jura, writing *1984*. Or a family telephone conversation in 2003, as folk in London demonstrated against preparations for war and a village in Mull mourned the death of one person. 'These moments' and 'Dancing alone' are about love and loss, written when a colleague died: lingering images from everyday experiences and conversations that can never be repeated. At the other end of life, writing words of welcome for my grandson, Thomas, I tried to reclaim familiar phrases for an experience that changes every family.

'The bell' and 'Candlemas' were written on Iona out of season, in winter: a time to look at things in a different way, with the possibility of fragile new beginnings. But it was a different kind of fragility that inspired 'The desert road' and 'Runcible birds'. Not long into a new stage of my life, I fell off my bike on a lonely back road in Mull, and almost lost that life.

When I recovered consciousness, for a time I could only see with one eye. But I hope these poems use both, and other senses – and the inner eye too. And I hope that they will speak to your condition, and your experiences – of letting go and holding on.

Jetty waking

Another little death:
a letting go
after the holding on
at the end of the jetty –
those clumsy hugs
and last words.

There will come a time
when you can't take
any of it with you;
but now, somehow,
you have to take it all:
bags, backpacks – all your stuff.

Another little death:
wading through the water
and, for those watching,
the ferry ramp closing
slowly, inexorably –
like curtains closing.

There will come a time
when we too will go this way:
crossing to the other side,
leaving the island of I.

But now, the world still asleep,
stand, salt spray stinging our eyes,
giving a good send-off, taking
leave, foolishly waving, weeping,
watching you out of sight, waking.

These moments

These moments
like windows into each other's lives –
sharing stories of a car
backing round the terrible cliffs of Gribun
in the small hours;
or a driver from the islands,
lost in city streets, hapless,
going round and round in Glasgow.
These moments of laughter:
these moments
turning over the words
'quality of life'.
These moments when eyes meet.

There was a moment today
on the edge of the village
when I met a deer on the road.
It sniffed the aromatic evening air,
and bounded into the trees –
gone in an instant.

There was a moment, too,
when we stood on your doorstep
listening together
to a thrush singing after the rain:
each cadence coming fresh –
aching with beauty.
In that moment, we stood on the edge
of a mystery, beyond words,
sharing the possibility
of a song that never ends.

Dancing alone

On a single-track road
the service bus is crossing the island:
its driver swinging round corners
with accustomed ease;
pulling into passing places,
as though steering a partner
through a ceilidh
in a crowded village hall.

He is keeping time
and he starts whistling a dance tune:
perfectly pitched, poignant,
the kind that works best for a last waltz.
Suddenly, spinning the wheel,
he has us all dancing –
his bus, every single passenger
and the passing hills reflected in the loch:
dancing together –
dancing alone.

George Orwell at Barnhill

Between death and death
he sat down to write a story.

Where the road ran out, he took to the track,
and at the track's end was a house
facing out to the sea –
with its beauty and danger,
its strange currents and paradoxes.

There he set up a small household
of vulnerable people, who had just the basics:
bare floors, hard beds,
a kitchen table, just enough chairs.
How did they get their groceries?
Water from the spring to brew tea.

For him it was the end of the line –
and he wrote about a man at the end of the line,
and a society breaking down.

He wrote through the dark rainy mornings
the still, midge-infested days and the nights cruel with stars.
Out of sight of the world of politics,
polemic, work, words, slogans, choices, compromises:
but it was all going on in his mind.
Watching. Watched.

A dying man in a damp house
sitting up in bed, with a blanket round his shoulders,
pounding his typewriter in the room above the kitchen –
beside himself with words –
while time was running out.

Beside his bed
a mug of tea going cold.

Slow walking

I'm aching, you said,
the day after the demo against the war,
so tired with slow walking:
It wasn't a march so much as a shuffle –
so many people packed into the city.
Yes, there was a common purpose,
a strong message, but
such slow walking
is very wearing.
And now, you said, all my bones are aching.

Remembered your words today
as six men carried a coffin
past my window:
slow walking
round the curve of the harbour,
past post office, fire station, pub:
six men keeping time,
honouring an appointment
with those who gathered for his funeral –
a whole community.

And, watching from the kerb,
I saw six fishermen
carrying the weight of death;
while – a long way from there –
demonstrators, you among them,
lifted up lovingly the life we share.

There's more than one way
of taking to the streets.
The aching in our bones
is both our mortality
and our yearning for life.

The heat of the kitchen

A woman works all day in the heat of the kitchen:
weighing, kneading, slicing onions thin,
shedding tears; stirring porridge with a spirtle;
tasting, judging the moment, pitching in,
finding the right words to encourage others,
burning her fingers, making sure all are fed;
and at last, weary – but knowing a job well done –
brings to the table fragrant, nourishing bread.

And that same night, in the expectant church,
stands to lead worship, and does it all over again.

There are days when she sits at the table,
eating with gratitude what others have prepared;
times in church when she receives with grace
others' serving, their savour of faith, their word.

So, tired at the end of the day, she rolls up her sleeves,
knowing how God keeps working in us like yeast,
taking her turn at the kitchen table of worship:
where work of ordinary folk becomes God's feast.

Home in Princes Street

Safe as houses –
but two-up, two-down
can barely contain
something so precious.

        Good as gold –
        but there is no price
        can be put on your life,
        on each breath.

Soft as silk –
the hairs on your head,
numbered; the skin
we caress with care.

        Wide as the world –
        your eyes, still to focus:
        everything is puzzling,
        all things are possible.

Proud as princes –
people becoming
part of your life:
trying on new roles, new names.

        Never the same again –
        a family changed
        as the world is changed
        by each child that enters it.

Lost for words –
when commonplaces are reclaimed,
two-up, two-down
cannot contain such wonder.

The desert road

This is my desert road:
this is where I fell among the stones.

This is where I set out,
in pride and self-sufficiency.

This is where I came to the hilltop
and began to freewheel downhill
with the wind in my hair
this is where I put the brakes on – too late –
this is where I rang my bell
this is where I fell.

And having failed the test in every way
this is where I lay:
in the mud, with the fragrance of bog-myrtle
blowing across the road
which had risen to meet me.

This is where
I shut my mind to my own story:
hid my eyes from happening and hurt.
This is where I lay intimately
with the stones, mingling blood

until neighbours came
and cared for me:
like ravens bringing bread,
like angels.

The runcible birds

They sit in a row
on the roof of the ward opposite –
migrating birds.
I cannot put a name to them:
watching with one eye,
my world having been turned upside down.

I think they have come
out of a book by Edward Lear –
runcible birds.

Just now it is enough that they are here,
and I'm keeping an eye on them:
not asking where they are going,
or their name by the book.
Simply keeping hold of reality
in all its rarity;
relishing the surprise –
the unasked-for gift –
of being alive
in a world turned upside down.

The bell

At first, I guessed
that its clangour was the cry of wild geese,
lifting off wet meadows,
resonant in the raw air
of a grey midwinter Sunday;

then I heard it was the dissonant beat
of the Parish Church bell,
rusting on its outdoor perch
at the gable end;

and I thought how it lacks the charm
of a chime of bells from a steeple
or the sonorous tolling of the Abbey bell,
ten minutes to each appointed hour;

but how, as it echoes from the crags,
uncompromising in its demand
that the people come –
with no promise of comfort or beauty –
we maybe hear
the gathering bell of a much older church,
the strange certainties of saints,
the urgency of the wild geese.

Candlemas

In the dark days:
under rain-heavy clouds,
among broken branches,
on sodden earth,
the snowdrops light their candles.

A flame that cannot be put out
by darkness or gales or doubt.

In the salt wind,
rooks buckle like broken umbrellas;
as the bare trees
heave a great sigh,
the snowdrops tremble.

But their flame cannot be put out
by darkness or gales or doubt.

Perfect, as though carved
in green-veined marble,
life pulsing through tissue
delicate as the eyelids
of a sleeping child,
curved like small fingers, holding on.

Their flame is steadfast:
darkness or gales or doubt
cannot put it out.

Figures in a landscape

Introduction

A sense of place runs through most of this writing. It's more than describing the landscape, it's about exploring the way that we live in it, are shaped by it, how our stories grow out of it, where we make connections. For instance, each time I travel on the West Highland Line I can't forget other, parallel journeys; I also glimpse other lives – maybe from something as transient as a headline in the *Oban Times*. At Loch Awe I remember the way my family gave eccentric names to places. As the Calmac ferry leaves Oban, time after time I see my father on the quayside ('Casting off').

Some of these are encounters on the edge of human experience: Side by side are a winter piece about Swinside stone circle in Cumbria, and 'Frink figures', written in Salisbury and London at midsummer, inspired by several of the sculptor Elizabeth Frink's compelling life-size sculptures. One is simply called 'Martyr' – how could I ignore the resonance of that word, just after the bombings in London in 2005?

Some of the poems in this section came out of a period as Writer in Residence at Southlands College, Roehampton University, mostly about that particular place. But a handful were inspired by different British landscapes, whose patterns – limestone pavements, the flow of water, the circles in felled tree trunks – can reflect or challenge our lives. We make different connections, different kinds of bridges – from an ancient clapper and arch over the Brathay in Little Langdale, to the great structures along the Tyne linking Newcastle and Gateshead – and we cannot be without bridges.

Loch Awe

'As though a boatload of Edwardian ladies went down here – leaving only their hats bobbing on the water …'

Dark, top-heavy,
with plumage of trees
pinned in place by Douglas fir:
these are the Hat Islands,
reflected in the still waters of Loch Awe
like Kilchurn Castle, Cruachan –
names in the public domain –
but this is just a family joke.

Naming them, my mother
maybe remembered her parents:
Frank, the warehouse clerk,
moustached, cutting a dash
in blazer and boater, and Jessie,
telephonist, in her best dress
and a once-in-a-lifetime hat
of heroic proportions –
both escaping the city,
with its narrow horizons;
crossing a rustic bridge,
captured by a travelling photographer
(after they paid him
there was no money left for the tea-room),

that moment, recorded
before the waters of time
swept them away,
leaving not even a hat.

Just islands, reflecting in still water
an inheritance of imagination and laughter.

Casting off

The man in shirtsleeves
spits on his palms,
eases the hemp collar from a bollard
on which someone has painted a smiling face.

A lifetime of casting off –
you taught us
to relish such moments,
you, who spent restless years
moving on,
leaving one safe quayside after another.

This was one port you left –
patrolling the Western Isles,
skipper of a small air-sea rescue boat –
at this point I cross your wake.

But I am making my own journey,
restless, still searching for a harbour
which will also be
a point of departure.

The last time I saw you
was on another quayside,
leaning on your stick,
watching the men loose the mooring ropes,
watching us, children and grandchildren,
growing smaller, waving, waving.

The man in shirtsleeves takes the looped rope
like a wreath and throws it across the space –
the dark water
growing wider all the time.

Travelling on Good Friday

Full moon on Good Friday:
like a wide-open eye
taking in landscapes of broken glass,
negatives, contradictions.

The 18.20 Glasgow-Oban train
full, too, of tired people –
home-comers without elation,
travellers in their separate worlds –

onlookers, in windows reflected,
eyes not meeting, unsleeping,
looking inward, but not weeping:
eyes turned away.

Past Faslane, the submarine pens
lit up like a fairground with no fun –
just deceptions – wall of death,
haunted house, hall of mirrors.

Past the wire fences of Glen Douglas
like the separation barrier
on the West Bank: a fine line
between security and insanity.

All irrelevant to the passing train
which moves on mundanely,
the passengers unmoved,
with their own thoughts safe inside.

But outside, all the way
on this Good Friday, cold light
reflects in mudflats, and still lochs,
from the white faces

of housing schemes and lonely crofts:
the full moon looking down
on a world of pain dry-eyed
wondering – can tears flow again?

West Highland Lines

Crime

Headline: a crime wave in Dalmally:
three Romanians put off the train there
because they couldn't pay the fare.
One, a mime artist,
also charged with unruly behaviour.

Mime

Ferns dance wildly as the train passes,
and clouds caress hill shoulders;
out there, a silent world
of small dramas, brief encounters
and hidden meanings.

Time

We are strangers passing through,
taking and making what we can –
of grand plan or green anarchy –
in a stolen moment of time,
seen through a glass wall.

Finding the stone circle

February, winter's last gasp.
On the day of the first celandine
we climb high above the estuary,
and, in a subtle fold of the hills,
gatecrash a gathering:

stumbling across the very stones
we set out to find –
having followed the map backwards
by tracks that became becks,
flinching from the knife wind,
misreading the signs –

but they were waiting all the time:
convened in the corner of a field,
fifty-five different stones, forming a circle
into which we step,
like children in a game.

Touch them gingerly, cold bones,
granite licked smooth by salt winds:
remembering Lot's wife, or tales of trolls
or cursed dancers, or a lodge
whose ceremony has its own logic.

A storytelling of stones.
Turning their backs to the wind,
they lean together like old men
in conversations we cannot catch.

The sky darkens; the snow comes,
whirling down from White Combe;
the stones cold-shoulder us
as we huddle against their lichened flanks,
gulping hot soup. Guessing.

They are preoccupied, listening
to music in another register –
a set of dancers poised
for a ceilidh beyond imagining.
A gap has opened in time.

We have no business here:
they are waiting for us to go.
Unbolt the gate, regain the track,
retrace our steps; the snow
stops.

Don't look back.

Frink figures

Caught on camera:
ordinary folk
going about their business
in an uneasy world.

A woman sets out,
purposeful, walking
towards the town –
someone's mother,
a down-to-earth madonna;
we can't read her mind.

A serious man
drives a flock of sheep
across a city square –
paternoster –
someone's father,
going to his daily work.

On the edge of vision,
about to step into the picture,
there's a lonely figure
labelled 'martyr' –
where does he fit in?
what does he want?
what's he about?

Caught on camera,
a group of men
setting off into the city –
each someone's son,
crossing common ground;
we know their purpose now
but can never read their minds.

Water under the bridge

Brathay, brawling and babbling
from the tarn down to the lake,
following a familiar course
between grassy banks and mossy stones,
silvery and sinuous,
in midstream meets a rock
which will not be budged,
and the silken strands of water divide,

some rushing to one side,
some cascading on the other:

Flowing under the clapper bridge,
the great slate slab
laid down like an ultimatum
between bank and rock;
or flowing under the arched bridge
of slates on edge, wedged in place,
rakishly raised eyebrow,
surprised over centuries.

Two ways of bridging,
spanning two streams
which have unravelled, become separate.

And, under the bridges, water
in mid-flow forced to choose,
or pushed by the momentum
of following water, goes left, right,
under the clapper, under the arch:
weed streaming in the current,
stones rolling with the spate,
water under the bridge,
going separate ways.

Then, only a few yards downstream,
merges again, plaiting the strands
that seemed separated for ever:
molecules mingled, currents reunited
with a grace that is beyond us.

But in our other element,
as we balance on clapper and arch,
crossing over, why should we feel regret?
All that has happened in our lives:
finding, losing, separating, choosing, moving on,
is water under the bridge.

River and bridges

Poem for a wedding

A river runs through the city –
from the high lonely moorland
where snow lingers
and curlews call,
to the huge, restless and future sea.

A river runs through the city –
over-arched by bridges,
between two proud places,
connecting North and South:
a place of meeting, communication.

A river runs through a city
pulsing with people's lives:
stories, memories, songs
then and now –
working lives and times of celebration.

A river runs through the city –
and keeps running through all of our lives.
But on this day,
in this particular place,
what you do declares
that we cannot be without bridges.

Caim – Kilmartin Glen

Fish rising break the stillness of a loch
And widening rings reach to the further shore;
The cup and ring marks on this lonely rock
Touch even those who wonder when, what for

Or who it was that carved them, what they tell.
Deep in the resined wood, a clean-cut tree
Records in rings the years until it fell:
A book axed open so that we can see.

The standing stones, aligned to stars that wheel,
Goalposts in mud, endure the winter rain;
Or, circled here, like dancers in a reel,
Wait on the caller, poised to move again.

We skim the surface, glimpse the power to bless
Of circles, caring and connectedness.

Clints and grikes

Clints, grikes – which is which?
No one is sure.
What's certain is that we're here,

on top of the world,
having scrambled up the dib
worn by meltwater from a glacier

long ago. Down there we clattered
over screes – white shards of stone
were dry as old bones;

clambered up from below ground,
as though through a manhole,
to stand on a limestone pavement.

Uncommon ground – crackled like ice,
a game of jacks, a scab on the hill's head,
a story cobbled together

of a giant's playground – though
the sky opens its arms here, we're wary,
watching our step among clints and grikes,

going slow, glimpsing little gardens
flourishing in each cleft, a thousand flowers
sheltered from the wind across the tops.

That wind catches our breath –
we look up, taking in the bigger picture,
edges, uplands, moors, like an ocean:

the world that we're on top of.
Think on, that's how we live our lives
most fully: looking outwards

towards the long horizons, the real world
that breaks on us like waves;
but anchored by feet on the ground,

earthed in specific time and space,
knowing that life has a different scale,
also real, in the crevices,

the secret places, the walled gardens
that flourish in such shared moments,
and in our hearts, open to the sky.

Conversations with Attie

Introduction

What follows was written in memory of Attie MacKechnie, born on the Ross of Mull in 1924. He died in 2005, and what I have written is not definitive, for many knew him longer and better than I did. But over a few years, while I worked in Iona, and then moved to Mull, I learned a great deal from visiting, and listening to him.

Attie's family were crofters, fishermen and quarrymen, working the granite of the Ross. After wartime service on the British/Russian convoys, Attie became involved, with other Gaelic-speaking craftsmen from the Ross, in the huge project of rebuilding the Abbey in Iona. He gave many years of his working life to this project, becoming a Member of the Iona Community, and eventually managing the Abbey Trustees' maintenance team. He was respected by both the ministers and laypeople of many traditions, who came for part of each year to work on the rebuilding, and by his neighbours in Bunessan and in Govan, where he worked as administrator for some time; in both places he was an Elder in the Parish Church. He was a man of great technical competence and personal integrity, full of energy and humour, and gifted in settling disputes. He knew how to build community.

One of the founders of the Ross of Mull Historical Centre, Attie was eager that the injustices of the Clearances, the endurance of Mull's people and the meaning of its place names should not be forgotten. He was a tradition-bearer. While many remembered his fine voice, singing at ceilidhs, he was also a storyteller, an outstanding *seannachie*.

Conversations with Attie

(In memory of Attie MacKechnie 1924–2005)

'I was brought up
to see ministers as awesome –
to respect the cloth. But I know now
everybody has a ministry.
It's up to you what you make of it.'
Schoolchildren, neighbours, ministers, friends,
outsiders, incomers, listened and learned.
Your words created community.

'The quarry houses at Camas
were salubrious, compared
to the small homes on the Ross of Mull,'
you said, whose family moved
from place to place,
from one small home to another,
from one township to the next,
within a few miles of bog and heather;
whose great-grandfather, on one side,
was a quarryman, a hammer-man
getting out the granite to build lighthouses;
another great-grandfather, the teacher
down at Uisken, stood up against
the powers of landlord and Kirk,
setting up Baptist worship in the school,
enraged the Factor, lost his home with his job,
lived in a cave, preached in the wilderness …
but then for his family's sake began again:
digging ditches, crofting, scraping a living,
built a home again, was moved on again –
as so many moved on. Shared their story.

'Solidly built, a sign of the Stevenson family's
meticulous care for their workers.'
You also were one who cared,
as Clerk of Works rebuilding the Abbey;
later, maintaining the fabric,
feet on the ground, part of a local team,
aware of bigger issues, a wider community;
caring for buildings and people, meticulous
about the things that make a difference.

'The Stevensons were very good
to their workmen.
Alan Stevenson once had a job to be done –
at Skerryvore or Dhu Heartach.
He pressed for it to be done on a Sunday.
Afterwards he apologised
to all the men individually.'
You told that story with understanding:
knowing the urgency of a job that must be done,
the power of local tradition,
the need for good workers to take real rest:
knowing that all men deserve respect.

'To be noble you have to be unpopular,'
you said about George MacLeod;
but you yourself were popular in many ways –
rooted in Mull, a Gaelic speaker,
related to half the Ross –
respected too, and much loved:
folk knew by experience that you
had found your ministry.

It was you who told us where
to look for the ruins of the old fishing hut,
or the standing stones, or the Baptist cave,
or the township from before the clearances,
or the roads and walls and pier built for oatmeal
in the hungry years; to know where
and to think about why they were there:
Seannachie, you fed folk with stories.

Simple stories: of the 'cuckoo piece'
that is the best way to start the day;
the true story of the quarrymen,
who walked from job to job,
with just their apron,
and their hammer in their hand;
complex stories of local injustice –
of Factor Mor, hated throughout the land;
a war story: when the cargo ship Ostend
exploded, lighting up the sky,
and hurling ashore bags of flour
which the sea had no time to spoil;
and from the same bay, the ancient tale
of Fraoch who fought the monster
of Eilean Ban and died for love,
with its heart grasped in his hand.

And a tale recalling when, in your lifetime,
laughing barefoot children
turned cartwheels under a full moon
on the strand, caught sand eels
and cooked them on a driftwood fire.

Educating with conversation
(rich with words like salubrious,
and meticulous,
and place-names and their meanings)
under-girded with the Gaelic;
blessing with song –
remembered from many a ceilidh;
nourishing with stories;
living with integrity.

*'Everybody has a ministry.
It's up to you what you make of it.'*

In this very place

Introduction

If, in the words of Irenaeus, 'The glory of God is in human beings fully alive,' that fullness of life doesn't happen in a vacuum, but with our feet on the ground in a particular place; our senses fully used, here and now.

And here and now I live on the Ross of Mull. This is where I stay, where I sojourn. In this landscape the changing seasons still make a difference, and the land and the people who live on it shape each other. This space on the edge – these great empty shores, village streets where neighbours meet, spring fires on the moorland, ruins, single-track roads, this mixture of rust and gold – is a place heavy with history, full of fantastical stories, present paradoxes. As I try to get my head round these, sometimes a poem is the most honest response I can make.

Iconic

Ben More drapes a pashmina of cloud
over her bare shoulder:
who says mountains are male?

On this lazy sunshine day
she smiles in a come-hither way;
but when the wind changes,
she could be a femme fatale.

What a picture – standing there just so,
waiting for the wind coming up the loch
to lift those full skirts of conifers
and miles of bog-myrtle –

she's laughing at us, sardonic,
larger than life, iconic:
our one-and-only Munro.

Tête-à-tête

Like pomegranate seeds
the street lights ripen
in the dusk, glowing red
then gold.

I cross the burn that's losing itself
in the bay; tide on the ebb,
winter light wrapping itself up,
going out.

Days don't get any shorter.
This time next year, the lost child
once more locked underground –
where will we be?

Now I carry in a brown paper bag
bulbs for friends who'll dib them
deep in the kind earth here,
watch them flower.

Handing it over, I fumble,
the bag breaks and tête-à-tête tumble
across the floor, shedding layers
of dry skin.

And we see how far from dead they are:
green shoots, unstoppable –
the light coming back,
the tide making.

All right, it was an eagle

All right
it was an eagle

because we know –
have been told –
of eagles there
among those crags, so
what else could it be?
Clearly a raptor
a big bird, with wide wingspan,
and it soared
in arrogant circles against the sun
with such freedom,

even far away we could feel
it playing with the wind.

If that wasn't an eagle,
then the eagles that we believe
are there, were somewhere else
at the time:
soaring in different skies,
delighting other eyes.

But of course it was an eagle
and I'll tell you why:

our little lives
narrow to what's safe and habitual;
hugging the ground,
we dare not live in case we die;
having wings,
we've forgotten how to fly

so we need eagles,
we need to see eagles,
we need there to be
eagles.

The Baptist cave – Ardalanish

What did you go out
into the wilderness to see?
A reed shaken by the wind?
Blackface sheep that stop and stare?
Cold waves falling on the long strand?
Brightness ebbing from the air?

Or this grey rugged stone
standing alone, scarred by time,
with lichen like wild hair.
With one fallen, part of a ritual long lost,
incoherent now: *Clachan nan Uamh*,
named not for its meaning, its why,
but its place in the world, its where.

In the cave behind, in an age
of less tolerance – or apathy –
a dissident preacher took refuge:
dismissed from his job,
turned out of a tied cottage with his family,
bedding down in bracken,
picking a living from the low-tide rocks,
preaching, Sunday by Sunday,
to a congregation of sheep, stones
and like-minded folk.

What did they go out
into the wilderness to see?

A man made articulate by faith and injustice;
hurling words into the teeth of the wind,
with a passion that kept them all warm.

Weather blether – climate change

Prowling round the house like a wolf
huffing and puffing in the chimney,
night-long: it's enough
to take your breath away –
a bad dream.

Surging through the forestry, making waves;
loud, angry, impatient: in your face;
it's ranting, chanting,
gallivanting all over the place
without rhyme or reason –
out of order.

Shaking sense out of a world
we've so far taken for granted,
so that trees grow horizontal,
waterfalls plume upward:
little wonder black-houses had round ends,
leaving no corner for the wind to lurk –
or get a grip.

Losing ours,
we close our eyes, huddle indoors,
hiding from stranger-danger,
hoping the wrath of God will pass over;
denying what we know in our bones,
what we're hearing –
the wind of change.

Second sight

You are the most here-and-now
person I know.

That is why you come to mind
when I am walking in the wind:
hearing it whispering in the sedge;
feeling the machair turf springy underfoot;
hearing the stones jostling at the sea's edge
and feeling them smooth and cold and hard;
hearing the curlews cry and breakers roar;
tasting salt, relishing a new word;
smelling the kelp tossed up along the shore

and seeing –
what you will see now vividly
in your mind's eye –
a double rainbow.

Somehow, when you're around,
there's double measure
and second helpings:
it is easy to feel twice blessed –
as cats with cream or pigs with clover –
to celebrate a glass more than half full,
a cup running over.

You are the most here-and-now
person I know.

A given day on Mull

After the storm
there came a day
as mild as milk –

the estuary flat calm,
herons rapt
in their reflections.

Where the sun
laid a warm hand
folk met in the street

and told the story of the wind's fury
through which each had travelled
alone in the dark –
barricaded behind doors
hail spitting on the windows
gusts booming in the chimneys.

Now, meeting face-to-face,
found being listened to
as sweet as honey.

Overhead, an eggshell sky
cloud-feathered, on still water
a raft of eider duck;

it was a given day,
intimate, precious and enduring:
like a painting on silk.

Muirburn

Like a sleeve
smudged across the page
to unwrite the record …

like a fuse lit,
spun wool unravelling,
clouds come down to earth …

like an army advancing,
a dream retreating,
an aftermath …

like a signal for help,
eyes blurred with tears,
ghosts coming and going on the moor …

a purging, laying waste,
a messy ending, making space;
death in the heart.

Yet, down there in the dust,
with blackened heather stems,
a glimmer of green –
a paradoxical fresh start.

Passing place

Two poets pass on the road,
each in a car
(the cars are unremarkable, are
a mere detail);
with careful craft
the drivers dovetail
on the narrow road,
finding a passing place;

these two folk –
whose minds are far from single-track –
what are they thinking,
each in their separate space
which keeps on moving?

One raises a hand, and
the other signals back
in wordless acknowledgement –
responding
like the tides to the moon's phases
or planets to each other's gravity –
but the momentum continues,
and the moment is gone.

Two poets pass on the road:
they wave
they travel on.

Rust and gold

Far off and long ago, Ibadan –
fabled city of rust and gold.
Here and now, in Iona, on Mull,
islands in the west of the world,
pan roofs catch the colour of dead bracken.
Here, aged vans, ploughs, boats
and machines whose use is forgotten,
rest, barnacled with rust.
Work of human hands being humbled,
crumbling back into earth.

Yet just now, the land's
extravagant with spring –
gorse kindling a fire on every hill,
king-cups brimming with pure gold.
And suddenly on a grey morning,
in a corner of an ordinary place,
a charm of goldfinches alight on a rusty wire fence,
scattering amber beads of rain
with outlandish grace.

Sigint, Staffa

On the cliffs of Staffa, we're listening in
to the private conversations of puffins
chuntering in their burrows.

Waves break below on basalt reefs;
along the cliff edge, predatory gulls patrol:
there is danger in the air.

But we are another species
and, for once, harmless
so the small birds trampoline up

clownlike and trusting,
with carryout fish suppers
for their hungry and hidden young,

bringing a taste of the wide world
to tales being told, underground,
with us listening in and standing guard.

After Thomas

I believe in the lark
although I cannot see it
against the sun –
suddenly so much April light
suffusing the moor,
where peat cuttings
and muirburn black
remember winter's long night;

now, a new beginning –
with this small bird
such a vital part,
overflowing the morning
with what feels like joy;
I paused on the worn track,
where the sound struck a spark –
now the long song
goes on, far beyond me,
shimmering out of sight;

beyond doubt, the lark
can be at once
sky-high and down-to-earth,
heard but not seen;
we need no written evidence,
nor eyewitnesses,
nor to be reassured by touch:

common sense –
here and now –
real presence
simply in the song.

Bird's-eye view

Like a couple of doves
cooried high on the Abbey tower,
look down with me now at green Abbey grounds,
graves in the Relig Oran, sheep grazing the crofts,

waves running down the Sound,
the busy ferry crossing over, white wings
of gulls, far islands ringing the horizon:
a whole little world, now look down.

Look there, two folk, hand in hand, slowly making
their way across the grass – how small they seem
from this height – but there is no mistaking
their togetherness, it fills the frame.

We are too far away
to see their faces, but if we could
Margaret's gentle smile would be reflected
in Jim's glasses, his laughter in her eyes.

We are too far away
to hear their voices, but if we could
it's likely they'd be sharing a joke, well-chosen words,
or the silence that says everything.

As it is, looking from afar, we can still see love
in the spring of their step, can recognise
two good friends who have been walking together
for a while now, and find it still makes sense:

walking together, gazing in wonder at God's world;
walking together joyfully, on common ground,
walking together simply, hand in hand,
walking together gently, on holy ground.

Kilvickeon

In this place of endings
and beginnings: of burial now
and baptism once upon a time,
foolishly gathered

in a roofless church –
which is also open-ended –
we gather to worship a God
of beginnings and endings.

Our singing and prayers,
under the sun and
carried by the wind, are offered
in the language of the Garden of Eden.

But Eden's the one place
where none of us are any more:
having moved on,
having lost so much,

barely knowing who we are:
pushed to the edge – or beyond –
folk who've wandered far
over the face of the earth,

formed communities
and seen them scattered,
built churches and seen them empty,
seen all fall into ruin;

now at home nowhere –
or everywhere – restless,
lost for words, or babbling
in a childhood tongue.

But still here we stand,
with our feet on the ground,
gathered for an hour under the sun,
between ruined walls:

singing and praying to a God
who is mysteriously present –
to whom our stories of exile,
songs of yearning, stumbling words,

even our tongue-tied silences,
taste of the feast to come,
and echo between these walls
the language of the Garden of Eden.

Broken china

A fine line
connects this tideline debris
with the story of our own lives.
It was the best china: tides of time
swept it away from the dark kitchen
and the well-kept dresser;
cleared the meal table once and for all
as the family scattered
across the world.

Now among wrack, stones, shells, strands of net
it winks a blue eye at us passing by,
the shore's homely, half-hidden treasure:
willow-pattern that has crossed
the bridge of no return.

And, like the last light
on the sea horizon as the sun sets,
from a fragment of gold rim
glimmers a clue to what we've lost,
something of great value
that is now beyond measure.

One day on the Ross

One day you wake
and the sky is a thin icy blue
and you hear the call of the wild geese,
with strong wing beats disturbing the air
as they land on the shore – but you
know they are only passing through.

One morning you glimpse
a green tide flowing –
transforming the hills, which winter
left pale and tired: the sap of spring rising;
but you know that seasons
keep turning, like waters coming and going.

One day you step
off the path, suddenly wading
through bluebells, fragrant and deep
in hue as the sky's zenith, primroses'
fine embroidery, violets like tiny jewels:
you know they're more precious, because fading.

One day you notice
the cuckoo has come and gone,
gold dandelions have turned into silver clocks,
seeds scattered, fledglings have flown the nest,
and different otters have reclaimed the shore:
like restless clouds, everything's moving on.

One afternoon, look,
reflecting the high-summer sky,
harebells fragile as joy, brief as a breath;
but you know they hold hope –
like that rainbow over the loch – being signs
(though dying) of love that will never die.

One autumn day –
when the burns are swollen with rain –
you see that the bracken's begun to turn;
rowan trees, glowing with ripe berries,
tell scarlet rosaries,
counting the days till winter comes again.

One day you look out
as gathering swallows, one by one, alight
on the wires like musical notes.
They played in the long movement of summer.
It comes to a close. They know
when it's time to go – and now the time is right.

Between high and low water

Between high water and low:
the space
that belongs to no-one – or everyone –
where there is no laird or factor
but only the oystercatchers
getting on with their lives;
where the nearest thing to a minister
is a reflective heron.

Salt marsh, sand and wrack:
the Kirk
of those whose conscience
drove them out of doors.

In imagination I watch them,
windblown preachers, moved by the spirit,
standing on damp sand
between high water and low,
or in a boat moored offshore –
the law cannot touch them there.

They know their Bibles, they know
that the powerful lose their grip,
wealth withers like bracken in autumn;
and they preach
a world turned upside down,
between high and low water.

On shakier ground, here I stand,
not quite belonging:
a sojourner between church walls,
struggling with structures,
crossing boundaries,
called to preach, but pulpit-wary;
respecting stubborn faith,
traditions with knotted roots like heather,

but wondering how we've ended up
weighed down like an old creel with sand.

Where pearls are still possible,
I'm grit in the oyster, maybe.
I leave
saltwater footprints on the nice carpets.

Shutting up the church – an empty shell –
for another week,
baffled Elders find strands
of seaweed in the aisle.

Out there,
someone's shouting into the wind
between low water and high.

Odd shoes

Introduction

If you want to understand someone, walk a mile in their shoes. This Native American saying started me on a difficult journey. For three months I walked several miles on dusty roads each day, accompanying men, women and children who left their home village to be confronted by the Separation Barrier, a high fence which cut them off from their land. My home is in the West of Scotland, but this was on the West Bank, in the Occupied Palestinian Territories, as a volunteer with the Ecumenical Accompaniment Programme in Palestine and Israel.

Three of us (an international team) lived in the village of Jayyous, and shared the lives of its people, mostly farmers. Our task was to monitor what happened daily at a checkpoint. The Separation Barrier being built by the Israeli Government around the West Bank diverges at that point from the internationally recognised Green Line by five miles. It has cut off 75% of the farmland of Jayyous. Only farmers with permits could get to their land; it was not clear how much longer that would be possible. They had to go through a slow humiliating process of having their IDs and permits checked, searches for weapons under their jackets and in the panniers on their donkeys. This is done by young heavily armed soldiers. What does this process do to each of them – Palestinian farmers, Israeli soldiers?

There as a 'non-violent presence', we watched and reflected on what we saw. I wrote reports and articles – and poems. Some expressed helpless anger; others celebrated the welcome and food we received from our neighbours – Aliah, who baked bread in the yard next door, or the Shatara family – and in simple open-air meals in the farmlands. Hospitality is at the heart of this culture.

Another tiny village, Yanoun, in the hills overlooking the Jordan valley, is surrounded by aggressive settlers. Ecumenical Accompaniers offer a protective presence. I was there during a few days of peace, during Eid, at the end of Ramadan. I picked olives there, as well as in the no-man's-land near Jayyous.

And the title? As part of our orientation to this complex situation the whole Ecumenical Accompaniment team visited Yad Vashem. The Holocaust Museum has a poignant pile of abandoned shoes. I remembered these, as I walked down to the barbed wire of the Security Barrier, and saw a single shoe lying at the roadside. Such pain. Such injustice. Then, now.

Odd shoes

There's always a single shoe –
on the tideline among the wrack,
or at the roadside, in the white dust –
perished leather, no laces, scuffed,
holes in its sole;
but it has a tongue:
what story could it tell?

> I took off my shoes
> – at the door of your home
> – where you worship
> – to walk on your land.
> I am watching where I tread:
> I am not worthy
> to be such a welcome guest.

In your shoes,
so well-worn,
so kindly lent –
what can I do?

> New shoes for a holiday,
> skipping in the dust;
> worn with the joy
> of being young and fully alive –
> not yet worn down.

So many shoes:
left behind
when, one by one,
alone and together,
you took that last step.

Belsen picture

Her mouth is open
in a silent shout.
Their mouths are all open:
for she is on top of a pile
of bodies tossed together –
too many to count.

But they do count:
each once a person with a name.

They are shouting to us
but we cannot hear
what they are saying,
or imagine
what scenes they witnessed,
what despair felt, what pain
brought them to this place.

There is a terrible repose
in their starved and stripped limbs
and at the same time
such an urgency in their faces –
their open mouths shouting to us
across the years.

And we both shrink away,
and strain to catch the words:

'Never again …'

       … never again?

The sea, the sea!

It was there all the time –
thirty-eight years –
more than a lifetime:
the sea, its salty tears
welling up in the western wind,
waves breaking
on long pale beaches under the sun – there
all the time, but unreachable
because of rusty wire,
settlers, guns, no-man's-land,
because of fear:
the waves there, breaking
just out of sight. And then,
the day came that you had waited for
all your short life: the way opened,
and you ran, ran,
kicking off your sandals,
pulling off your shirt,
into its arms.
But it was a stranger.
Its cold welcome took your breath away
and, at that moment of freedom,
it took your life.

Quick

The sun is rising
slowly
throwing into sharp focus
what happens at the checkpoint:
a petty process –
humiliation in the name of security –
carried out deliberately,
slowly.
Then a young man
who has submitted his ID,
his permit, submitted to scrutiny
from someone his own age,
but with a gun;
has answered questions,
and had his donkey cart
checked for explosives;
is waved through at last,
slowly.
So he urges his donkey
into a trot, along the military road
with the rising sun in his face;
then
they break into a gallop
as though, in this moment,
they could break out
of all these constraints,
denial, oppression –
this slow death of the spirit –
galloping into the sun
of a new day.

Rite of passage

She is twelve and a half,
has become a woman
is wearing the *hijab*
demurely, with a cerise blouse
that looks new and rather special, too,
for a day in the farmlands picking olives,
along with a bounce of little brothers and sisters,
swinging their pails on a day off school.
She walks down the dusty road
wearing her new identity with grace.

But she does not have a permit.
Between child and woman she is caught out,
stopped by the soldiers,
and stands still in the gateway
in her pink blouse and *hijab*,
while her father pleads
and her sisters and brothers run ahead
among the olive trees.

Then she has to turn
and walk slowly back home
up the steep dusty track, stretching ahead:
at this turning point in her life
having no right to pass.

How to strip an olive tree

First, call friends, neighbours;
next, approach the tree,
with its cascading leaves like tears
and its clustering ripe fruit, green or black;
next, spread your cloths under the tree;
next, beat the tree (the way you might beat a donkey);
next, comb the branch-tips with your fingers,
till the olives fall pattering all around you;
next, use ladders to reach higher,
work together;
next, send small boys up the tree;
next, watch as they beat the higher branches
so that olives fall like hail;
next, the children edge out along the branches,
and their small weight tips the balance
so that laden branches
bend into the hands of the pickers;
next, check that the tree is stripped;
next, sit down in its shade
and drink hot sweet tea out of a kettle,
share bread and oil and herbs –
and olives of course;
next, put kindling aside;
next, with many hands, take up corners of cloth,
gathering the fallen olives together;
next, scoop the fruit and leaves into a bucket,
lift it above your head, pour it out, winnowing,
repeat;
next, scoop your olives (leaving the leaves) into a sack;
next, fold the cloths away;
next, glean the fallen fruit;
next, look up into the branches,
stripped bare of fruit, and say,
'That's a fine tree, old, but year by year, good fruit';
now move on; next …

Aliah bakes bread

She rose before dawn,
mixed the dough,
kneaded it in her neat home,
folded it like clean sheets
and set it aside,
to rise in its turn.
> Aliah woke her family
> and fed them,
> carried water, washed floors,
> left everything in order.
But now she is sitting
in her blue dress
in the bakehouse in the yard,
that ramshackle shelter
against rain and sun,
among the ashes of old fires,
while, in the iron stove, the new fire
for the new bread burns bright.
> The dough is pliant, alive,
> latent and, right now,
> resting under a cloth
> faded with much washing
> and drying in the sun.
Roots and knots of olive wood,
hauled from the hillsides,
are piled ready to feed the fire.
> She swings out the griddle –
> which holds the heat of today's fire,
> and years of sunshine
> on the olive trees –
takes a disk of living bread
in her quick hand and
tosses it onto the hot metal.

At once it blows up –
a puffed pitta, a bread balloon!
      Watchful, smiling, using a long spoon
      as though supping with the devil,
      Aliah turns the bread, lets it brown,
      bake through, and then, deftly,
      lifts it out to cool. Loaf by loaf
the pile grows, its warm aroma
wafting into the street; children
peep round the gate; neighbours
arrive to pass the time of day,
standing the heat of this kitchen,
approving the way she provides
for her household. They feast
on it with their eyes; some taste:
companionable work, baking.
      The last disk of dough,
      tossed onto the hot griddle
      by hands swift and skilled,
      is watched intently, turned,
      not allowed to burn.
      There is no waste.
The fire dies down, but warmth
lingers in the loaves, to be
passed on in nourishment.
      Among the ashes – see
      where there was no bread –
      enough fresh loaves to feed a family:
      enough to share, enough to give away.
And the fire still glows
in Aliah's face; right now
the making of bread
is her mystery; right now
she is skilled and fulfilled.
      Right now
      there is bread for today.

Under the lemon tree

Under the lemon tree
there is a table spread:
a place of hospitality
and breaking bread.

From the garden, ripe fruit:
pomegranate, fig, pear;
round the table, friends meet,
blessed to be there.

Fresh olive oil, soul food,
sweet pastries to share:
O taste and see that God is good;
know that God is here.

Yanoun I

In her low doorway, an old woman
swings a goatskin to and fro,
slowly churning goat's milk:
shuff shuff shuff –
patiently making cheese –
shuff shuff shuff.

Cats crouch hungry on the step,
sheep blether in the fold,
November sun has a hard edge,
the evening air grows cold;
and the pale stones underfoot
are rough, rough, rough.

Along the track, a small boy
scuffles, in big sandals
and hand-me-down clothes:
shuff shuff shuff –
struggles along in grown-up gear –
shuff shuff shuff.

'What to do?' crows the cock;
'Endure, only endure,' the donkey brays;
and the shepherd's dog, brusquely,
has the last word:
'Enough … enough … enough.'

Yanoun II (small change)

All quiet for once, the morning aired and ironed:
these busy households resting for a spell;
only a rooster crowing, and rusty bells
of sheep being watered at the village well.

Dressed in new clothes for Eid, the children skip
(being simply safe) along the village street,
clutching small change, laughing and buying sweets;
and elders take the sun, and families meet.

And then the silence breaks, the valley shakes:
not guns but fireworks, as the people share
defiance – though the watchers are still there –
hearing and tasting freedom in the air.

Nargis

In no-man's-land –
between the Green Line
and the razor wire;
in the sequestered farmlands,
between two peoples;

in no-woman's-land –
between olive and almond trees
with bitter fruit, among the wild thyme;
between white rocks
and red earth;

in no-child's-land –
cut off from school and friends
by high fence and shut gate,
and by the eyes of soldiers;

between summer and winter,
and after the first rains,
springing up among the stones,
the small wild narcissus
fills the air with sweetness
that overwhelms: the fragrance
of something lost forever –
but not forgotten.

Another landscape

Introduction

I was a sojourner in the West Bank, too – and this place was both unfamiliar and deep under my skin. My eye and mind were taking in Middle Eastern landscapes which resonated with those of the Pennines and Hebrides – the same geology, but a different climate and history; land farmed in different ways, yet with outcrops of rock or human gestures which I recognised, in another context: like the universal spread-arms gesture of a boy herding sheep.

I also found myself reading passages from the Bible with different eyes. I had entered the closed city of Nablus and, in the midst of the struggle going on in that region and in people's daily lives, drew water from Jacob's Well, aware of my own striving to glimpse God in such darkness and complexity.

Two of these pieces were written in successive years as Advent meditations. I was still wrestling with the experience of living for a few months on the West Bank, and then leaving behind people who had been my neighbours, as they made heroic efforts to go on living normal lives in a continuing crisis, under oppression and in poverty. 'Terminal' was in fact written on Christmas Eve, two days after returning to Britain, as I asked angrily: 'How can we sing carols in a comfortable church, while there's a wall being built round Bethlehem?'

From the hard rock, fresh insights; from an ugly 'terminal', the meaning of incarnation; from a tree destroyed by injustice, a new shoot; from a dark well, living water. In the otherness of this landscape, God is powerfully present.

Basalt

Not only here:
the strange symmetry of creation
outcropping in such different places,
taking us by surprise.

In the Hebrides, on the world's edge,
basalt islands, where puffins
burrow and breed: their domesticity
taking for granted God's geometry.

In Galilee – did folk see themselves
as on the edge or at the centre? –
the dark rocks of Capernaum
built homes, markets and synagogues.

Time has taken the roof off the town,
its community long since left the nest;
but the stories echo in our minds
like sea-music in a cave.

On this low ground, beside an inland sea,
columns forged in outlandish fires:
borrowed to build ordinary homes
in a small town, strangely familiar.

Was it here God entered human history,
taking us by surprise?
Not only here.

Banyas
(Matthew 16:13–20; Mark 8:22–37)

This is where they came:
to this cliff-face, its ancient strata
still rippling, long after the earth shook;
this rainbow of striations: minerals
leaching out of the earth, elemental;
this womb-like cave; this place
with temples to flawed humanity
and the strange cult of dancing goats;
this overhanging cliff (along its edge, look,
a boy leading his flock): a cliff-face
where pastoral images echo with panic …

To the foot of this cliff, they came:
those following friends full of questions
for a teacher, who stopped right here, asking:
'Who do men say I am?'
Names came to their lips:
mythic figures from the past
looming in their minds like hewn statues.
'And you, who do you say I am?'
One fumbling, found the words,
'Messiah,' he said, 'Son of the living God!'
Words celebrated ever since, set in stone,
and Peter affirmed with a new name.
So on this rock, this compromised,
too-human, crowded and crumbling rock,
the Church was built. At this cliff-face,
and still from place to place to place.

But all the time
the truth was even closer than the rock,
the truth was springing up under their feet:
the answer, without needing words,
was in the syllables of flowing water,
with light on it, water dancing and singing;
water, flowing out from under the cliff-face
(the crumbling rock and ruinous structures) –
flowing out freely, daring to go much further,
ready to bless the land; the gift of grace,
challenging dry certainties; refreshing,
meeting the need of thirsty folk; revealing
the way God's Spirit works:
pure and profound and down-to-earth.

Yanoun III

Limestone country:
pale rocks, scars, caves,
pavements, clints and grikes,
hillsides crackle-glazed.
> Hard-edged, and between
> the white knuckle-bones,
> instead of tender green grass,
> a grey thorny scrub.
Instead of larks, eagles;
instead of hawthorn, oak, ash:
almond, fig and olive trees;
drystone walling turned to terraces.
> Limestone country
> that glaciers never shaped,
> knowing its own seasons, farmed
> otherwise, history still being told.
A silent witness of white rocks;
instead of windmills, watchtowers
on the high tops overlooking Jordan;
after the rain, different flowers.

And it was like this
(Genesis 18:1–14)

And it was like this:
there was a family in a stony wilderness.
They had set up a tent, a hut, a shed –
something temporary –
a shelter for people just passing through,
but it was also home,
and they had roots in that place.

Nor was it wilderness: look closely,
the stones had been heaved aside
to find fertile earth,
and there was water flowing
and trees growing, bearing fruit,
also a garden under the trees
with just enough beans, okra,
greens, to feed the family day by day.

They were travelling light
but, for now, resting in a God-given place.
And it was like this:
fasting through the long dry day
until nightfall, but when the strangers came –
in the shimmering heat of midday –
they prepared food to set before their guests.

This is how the story goes:
Hospitality, blessing and laughter
and the birth of a child:
and somewhere a promised land.

But before all the confusions about land
and the question of sharing it,
long before, comes this sacrament
of welcoming the stranger,
in the stony wilderness that's also a garden,
in the shed that's also a home:
a table set with home-made cheese,
olives, food from the garden, bread and mint tea
prepared and offered with care
by fasting people for hungry strangers:
and it was like this.

Jacob's Well

(John 4:4–29)

The well is deep – forty metres –
and no longer under the open sky;
there's a dome over it,
a basilica still being built,
a shrine underground, around the well.
It is so deep,
inside this dim sanctified space,
and so far back in our minds,
that though we can lean on the parapet
and peer down, peer back in time,
it is all dark:
we cannot glimpse the water.
It is hard to see what this is all about.

It's so deep
we will need a bucket.
But right here, beside the well,
there's one waiting:
not a ritual vessel,
not a historical reconstruction,
just a shiny galvanised bucket
with a rope and a windlass.
Because the well is deep.

We let the bucket down,
and for a long unwinding time,
creaking, clanking, it descends.
It takes minutes: the well is deep …
and then a distant splash
and a pull on the line like a fish hooked.
Far down it finds water and sinks,
drinks, fills, ready to be hauled up,
out of the depths.

Heavy now: we have to push
against the pull of its weight on the windlass,
while the sound of water tipped
from the swinging bucket
echoes in the farthest reaches of the well.
Then – like the blink of an eye –
a lamp in the shrine shines back
from the brimming bucket still far below:
light reflected, a little light going a long way;
shimmering like quicksilver,
darting in the dark like a fish;
surprising, rising into the light of day;
recollected, like something we had lost
restored; coming back into our lives:
living water from a deep well.

The shepherd

On the next hillside
sheep grazed,
searching out the few green shoots
among stones and thorny scrub:
a vulnerable flock
on the move, lean beasts –
hunger on four legs –
their dusty fleeces
grey-brown like the land.

Overhead a bird of prey
hovered on desert thermals
wings spread, watchful.

The shepherd boy
stretched out his arms, guiding the sheep
away from a sheer drop,
and glimpsed the same thing happening
one hill further on,
where a man hung on a cross.

Keeping hope alive

The steadfast olive tree,
at home on the hillside,
at the door of the house,
is a silent witness.

Gnarled trunk, knuckled limbs
telling the tale of years,
grey-green leaves quivering like laughter –
leaves shaped like tears.

Frugal, it flourishes in poor soil:
generous, it nourishes the people:
bearing fruit in season,
yielding healing oil.

Its roots hold together dry earth,
branches give shelter from the sun:
it clothes the land:
it is rooted in the land.

It is a promise of peace.

Needed and taken for granted,
it stands for the future of the people.

What is left when it is gone?

Now, when homes are destroyed
and a way of life is swept away,
the olive trees are uprooted,
hillsides are bare – what is left?

A fragile sapling planted
close against the fence
that divides the land
and threatens mortal danger:

an olive tree taking root,
grey-green leaves flickering in the wind,
under the sun, a silent witness:

maybe
                a sign of hope.

In no-man's-land
(Job 14:7–9)

The bulldozers were here a year ago,
destroying an olive grove,
uprooted trees, leaves shed out of season
and crushed limbs scattered on the earth.

As young trees were taken away
for replanting in settlements,
soldiers kept back the farmers:
'When I saw my olive tree
dancing in the jaws of the bulldozer,
then I wept.'

The torn earth still lies bare,
a military zone now, a no-man's-land.
What will happen next?
The people wait, steadfast and sad,

and life goes on – strangers are welcomed,
families need to be fed:
branches of the felled trees
fuel backyard ovens, baking daily bread.

Under the moon, behind locked gates
in the farmlands, wild pigs trample and devour
crops that cannot be harvested; a white jackal
runs like death among coils of razor wire.

But under the sun
something is being unlocked
in the desert that was once an olive grove:
from the root, the ravaged stock
of an ancient tree
that seemed gone for ever –

a shoot growing, tender leaves unfolding
like a child's opening hand:
against all despair, a new beginning,
even here, even in no-man's-land.

When I saw it, I wept.

Terminal

(Luke 2:1–20; Isaiah 9:2)

So that's it then.
The logical conclusion.
Bethlehem sealed off
from the world by a concrete wall.
Of course there's still a way through:
no longer a checkpoint;
something much more civilised –
a terminal.

Not a terminus:
things don't end here –
don't be ridiculous!
Think of an airport:
passengers processed, due procedures,
security, a streamlined system,
efficient, hygienic.
Please keep this terminal clean.

White wall, polished floors,
glass booths. Bullet-proof.
Please follow the instructions.
Failure to do so may result
in your being turned back.
It's for your own safety.

Pilgrims with passports one way.
Other people, huddled humanity,
have got used to queuing; coming and going
with difficulty between home and work,
home and school, home and hospital:
Hard, if Bethlehem is home.

The jostling crowd watch the time,
talk to each other, complain, listen,
laugh at absurdities, look anxious,
shrug helplessly, wait wearily
for the red light on the turnstile gate
to click to green; then, one by one
(not with their neighbours,
parents separated from children)

each is allowed through the cage,
to the X-ray machine,
goes through that,
waits while bags are checked,
standing still, under surveillance
from armed soldiers on a catwalk above.
They walk forward, one by one,
to the booth with the bullet-proof glass
to show their IDs, and the permits
to continue lives in the world outside.
There's no eye contact.
A sterile environment. Minimum risk.

Catching the bus for Jerusalem
a man, at the end of his patience, exclaims
'This bloody checkpoint!'
Thank God for human emotion
and honesty, which refuses
to keep this tidy solution clean.

Or let this terminal
be a euphemism for humiliation,

and the fear which only gets more
when people on two sides
cannot look each other in the face.

Crossing this polished floor,
how far we've come
from the baby born on the earth
of a stable, among straw and dung;
among human voices and animal warmth.

Herded through pens,
how different our journey
from the local shepherds,
who came and went freely
to see with their own eyes
and to share good news.

Caught between gates and guns,
how far from the angels
who proclaimed peace on earth
to all people of goodwill –
even though the official sign outside
tells us *Have a good day.*

But this is still Bethlehem,
just one place in an unjust world,
where the people stand
on common ground, with little hope.
And where God is present, incarnate,
in the arms of a woman
like you or me
standing at a closed gate
waiting for the light.

Not cursing the darkness

Introduction

Each Advent, for the last few years, I've spent time reflecting in silence on the images and issues that have been with me during that year. After silence, the words come. Here is one such meditation. It was written out of the experience in Iona – which many readers of this book may have shared – of lighting candles in the Abbey Church as an act of witness, a sign of commitment, and then carrying them out into the draughty cloisters, or further still, into the open air, into the world.

At this point worshippers in Iona become one with others holding vigils, making prayer visible – in the heart of London, at Faslane, at many other places in a world of suffering and injustice.

'It is better to light a candle than to curse the darkness.'

Carrying a candle

Carrying a candle
from one little place of shelter
to another
is an act of love.

To move through the huge
and hungry darkness, step by step,
against the invisible wind
that blows for ever around the world,
carrying a candle,
is an act of foolhardy hope.

Surely it will be blown out:
the wind is contemptuous,
the darkness cannot comprehend it.
How much light can this tiny flame shed
on all the great issues of the day?
It is as helpless as a newborn child.

Look how the human hand,
that cradles it, has become translucent:
fragile and beautiful; foolish and loving.
Step by step.

The wind is stronger than this hand,
and the darkness infinite
around this tiny here-and-now flame,
that wavers, but keeps burning:
carried with such care
through an uncaring world
from one little place of shelter to another.
An act of love.

The light shines in the darkness
and the darkness can never put it out.

Appendices

Iona Community Justice and Peace Commitment

We believe:

1. that the Gospel commands us to seek peace founded on justice and that costly reconciliation is at the heart of the Gospel;
2. that work for justice, peace and an equitable society is a matter of extreme urgency;
3. that God has given us partnership as stewards of creation and that we have a responsibility to live in a right relationship with the whole of God's creation;
4. that, handled with integrity, creation can provide for the needs of all, but not for the greed which leads to injustice and inequality, and endangers life on earth;
5. that everyone should have the quality and dignity of a full life that requires adequate physical, social and political opportunity, without the oppression of poverty, injustice and fear;
6. that social and political action leading to justice for all people and encouraged by prayer and discussion, is a vital work of the Church at all levels;
7. that the use or threatened use of nuclear and other weapons of mass destruction is theologically and morally indefensible and that opposition to their existence is an imperative of the Christian faith.

As Members and Family Groups we will:

8. engage in forms of political witness and action, prayerfully and thoughtfully, to promote just and peaceful social, political and economic structures;
9. work for a policy of renunciation by our own nations of all weapons of mass destruction and for the encouragement of other nations, individually or collectively, to do the same;
10. celebrate human diversity and actively work to combat discrimination on grounds of age, colour, disability, mental wellbeing, differing ability, gender, race, ethnic and cultural background, sexual orientation or religion;
11. work for the establishment of the United Nations Organisation as the principal organ of international reconciliation and security, in place of military alliances;
12. support and promote research and education into non-violent ways of achieving justice, peace and a sustainable global society;
13. work for reconciliation within and among nations by international sharing and exchange of experience and people, with particular concern for politically and economically oppressed nations.

Putting these poems to work

What a strange concept! Shouldn't poems just be allowed to *be* – like the lilies of the field which neither toil nor spin? However, over the last few years quite a few of the pieces in this book have been woven into the fabric of acts of worship, workshops, pilgrimages. So here are some things you could try at home – with these or any other poems. There's life beyond the printed page …

A workshop: Several of the poems in 'A Gathering' have been used in a workshop on the Book of Kells. We included a showing of the Trinity College Dublin video *The Work of Angels*, a chance to look at postcards and books that reproduced some of the artwork, a hands-on session on calligraphy and uncial script, and encouragement to do some creative writing. My poems were not a model, but an example of one person's response to the riches of these manuscripts and their story.

A glimpse of the Holy Land: Visits (though not many) to Israel/Palestine, a placement as an Ecumenical Accompanier, and the need to share these experiences, mean that many of these poems are set in that troubled region, describe specific incidents or attempt to capture insights. They could be used as part of an evening with a peace and justice focus, combined with a showing of a good DVD (for instance Mohammed Alatar's *The Iron Wall*, available from Friends of Sabeel UK) or maps and photographs. I have used my own, but Christian Aid and other organisations could provide sets. I have also used a painting of an olive tree as an 'ikon', to accompany the poem 'Keeping hope alive' – or objects made of olive wood, to be passed around. A vase of anemones can be placed in the centre of the group for a reading of 'The flowers of the field', followed by a silence.

Flyposting: A few of these poems were produced as polemic – as were others written during the Residency in Southlands College. Around the campus they were 'flyposted' on noticeboards and glass doors, or photocopied as fliers and left on tables in the canteen, along with all the ephemera of student life. There might be a place or an event where you feel moved to do the same with one of these poems – or one of your own. Just make sure, if you print something out, to give (or claim) credit.

Round a table: A poetry reading doesn't need a person on a platform. How about gathering friends for a simple meal, then reading poems – these and others – to each other? You could choose a theme beforehand – food, even (see 'Bananas', 'The heat of the kitchen', 'Under the lemon tree', 'Aliah bakes bread' …).

Bible study: Some of the poems were inspired by an Old or New Testament story. What emerged was not in-depth exposition, but a different way of looking at a passage, which could be one element in a Bible study opening discussion of linked issues. Look at 'And it was like this' (Genesis 18:1–15); 'In no-man's-land' (Job 14:7–9; Isaiah 11:1–5 and maybe Isaiah 5:1–7, too); 'Banyas' (Matthew 16:13–20; Mark 8:27–33); 'Jacob's Well' (John 4); 'St Peter Gallicantu' (Matthew 26:69–75; Mark 14:66–72; Luke 22:54–62); 'Carrying a candle' (John 1:1–5).

Worship and reflection: Worship – our offering to God – is much more than what happens in church on Sunday. It is also an impulse underlying many of these poems. And, although none were written for specific acts of worship (unlike the monologues and biblical reflections in *Out of Iona*), quite a few have ended up being used in liturgy: 'Were you there?' 'Via Dolorosa', 'The shepherd', 'After Thomas'. As you read them, you may find others that will be relevant to gathered worship, as well as personal reflection.

Twitching: This is a bit of fun, really. I'm not a serious bird-watcher, but there are (for various reasons) a great many birds in this volume. In an idle moment see how many you can spot (don't forget the publisher – Wild Goose)!

Pilgrimage: Many of these poems are about place – and you will know (maybe by heart) others by greater writers, which celebrate a particular place known to you or capture the spirit of a river, a ruin or a hilltop. Plan a 'poetry pilgrimage', with a group, and take with you poems (maybe some of these, like 'Clints and grikes', for instance) which will connect where you pause to reflect with other places, and with the inner journey which we are also making, all our lives.

Dedications

Many of these poems were originally written for particular people who have inspired me, who helped me see a place with fresh eyes, or whose turns of phrase started a poem rolling. I sent the resulting words by email, on postcards, in pamphlets, or read them aloud to you. Maybe you recognise them now because they describe stories of which you were part, places that are significant to you. The common ground of these pages, like sand printed by birds' feet, is covered by patterns of words which belong to you, too.

Ethel, Alfred, Anna, Don,
David, Karen, Katy, Tom,
Meg and Paul and Barbara,
Adomnán, Victoria,
Emily, Effie, Hughie, Sue,
Nancy, Gordon, Alan too,
Sharif, Siham, Margaret, Jim,
Attie, Peter, Brik and Bill,
Judith, Derek, Jen and John,
Karen, Afaf, Andreas, Trond,
Ruth, Patricia, Ruth again
Dwin, Joy, Ian, Janna, Jane,
Runa, Helen, Abi, Mark,
Peter, Sarah, Stewart, James
Aliah, Lesley, Eleanor,
Maggie, Ronnie, Andy, Jenny,
Pauline, Maureen, many names:
I've so much to thank you for;
I've so much to thank you for.

Jan Sutch Pickard

Credits

Many of these poems originally appeared in pamphlets produced by Oystercatcher Publications in the Gatherings series: *A Gathering, Holy Places, Letting Go … and Holding On, Duck-density, Odd Shoes, Salt and Sweet* and *Carrying a Candle*. A number, written while Writer in Residence at Southlands College, were published as *Flight Path* (Roehampton University, Southlands Methodist Centre). 'Casting off' was first published in *Pushing the Boat Out* (Wild Goose Publications) and several other poems in later anthologies from Wild Goose. Some appeared in print first in *Coracle*, the magazine of the Iona Community.

The Iona Community is:

- An ecumenical movement of men and women from different walks of life and different traditions in the Christian church
- Committed to the gospel of Jesus Christ, and to following where that leads, even into the unknown
- Engaged together, and with people of goodwill across the world, in acting, reflecting and praying for justice, peace and the integrity of creation
- Convinced that the inclusive community we seek must be embodied in the community we practise

Together with our staff, we are responsible for:
- Our islands residential centres of Iona Abbey, the MacLeod Centre on Iona, and Camas Adventure Centre on the Ross of Mull

and in Glasgow:
- The administration of the Community
- Our work with young people
- Our publishing house, Wild Goose Publications
- Our association in the revitalising of worship with the Wild Goose Resource Group

The Iona Community was founded in Glasgow in 1938 by George MacLeod, minister, visionary and prophetic witness for peace, in the context of the poverty and despair of the Depression. Its original task of rebuilding the monastic ruins of Iona Abbey became a sign of hopeful rebuilding of community in Scotland and beyond. Today, we are about 280 Members, mostly in Britain, and 1500 Associate Members, with 1400 Friends worldwide. Together and apart, 'we follow the light we have, and pray for more light'.

For information on the Iona Community contact:
The Iona Community, Fourth Floor, Savoy House, 140 Sauchiehall Street,
Glasgow G2 3DH, UK. Phone: 0141 332 6343
e-mail: admin@iona.org.uk; web: www.iona.org.uk

For enquiries about visiting Iona, please contact:
Iona Abbey, Isle of Iona, Argyll PA76 6SN, UK. Phone: 01681 700404
e-mail: ionacomm@iona.org.uk

For books, CDs & digital downloads published by Wild Goose Publications:
www.ionabooks.com